THE GOLD EGG

BY ULE B. WISE

Copyright ©2017 Dan Wyson – Published by Ule B Wise Publishing
All rights reserved. No part of this book may be reproduced in any form
or by any means without permission in writing from the Publisher.
International copyright secured

In the land of Pertuffle, in the valley of Nopp

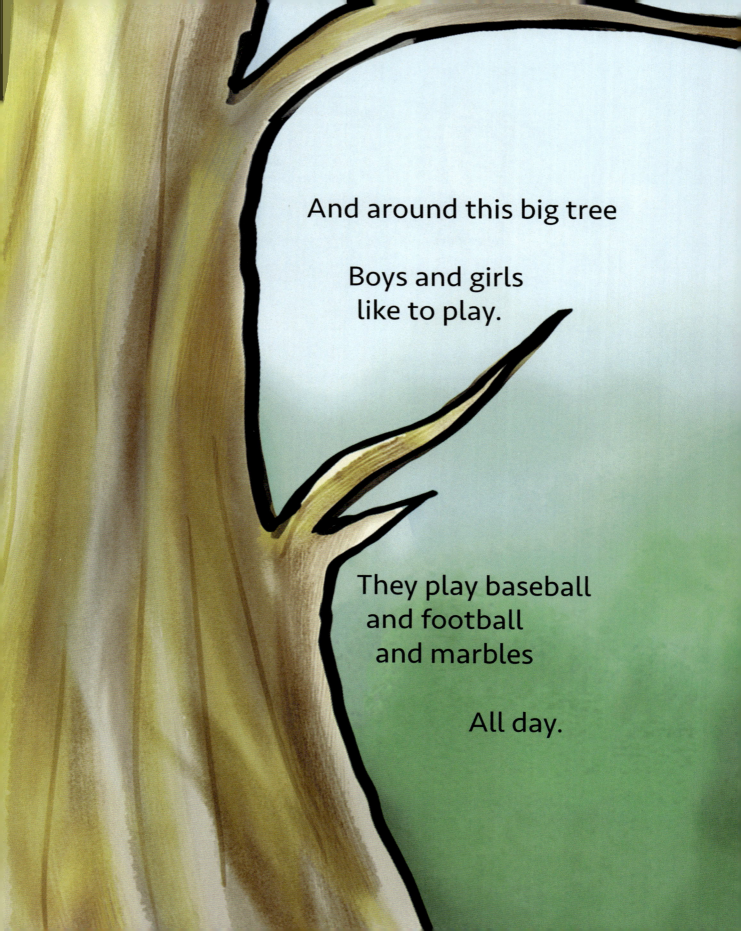

When the sun's shining bright
and the weather's too hot,
do you think they keep playing?
Why no, they do not.

But instead
they all sit in the cool of the shade
and they brag like kids do
while they drink lemonade.

One day while they sat looking up at the sky,
An elderly man with a cane happened by.

Now the children, amused
with what they just heard

'Bout a pure golden egg
in the nest of some bird,

Started in one by one
making fun of the man,

While they laughed and they teased
the old man with the cane

Making fun
of the story he told them that day

Near the trunk of the tree
stood a small boy named Devan,

Who said not a word,
he just gazed up towards heaven.

It was so very high up,
he could just barely see
the Kloonee bird nest in the top of that tree.

And though only a fool
would have wasted his time...

Devan grabbed the first branch
and he started to climb.

"Come back down," yelled his friends,
"You are foolish to try.
You never could climb to that nest,
it's too high.

And besides, what's the use?
There's no gold in that tree.
There never has been
and there never will be."

And though Devan supposed
they were probably right,
still he grabbed the next branch
and he held to it tight.

Then he pulled himself up,
inch by inch up the tree.
"If there's gold in that nest,
I will have it," said he.

Then suddenly "CRACK,"
what a terrible sound. As a branch broke
young Devan came tumbling down.

His friends rushed to help the bruised boy in the dirt.
"Are you well? Are you whole?
Can you see? Are you hurt?"

As he lay on his back Devan spoke not a word.
He just looked at the tree
toward the nest of that bird,
wondering to himself what his next step would be,

Wondering,
"Was a gold egg worth climbing that tree?"

But they all were surprised
as he wiped off the dust
and he said,

"I must climb to that Gold Egg, I MUST!"

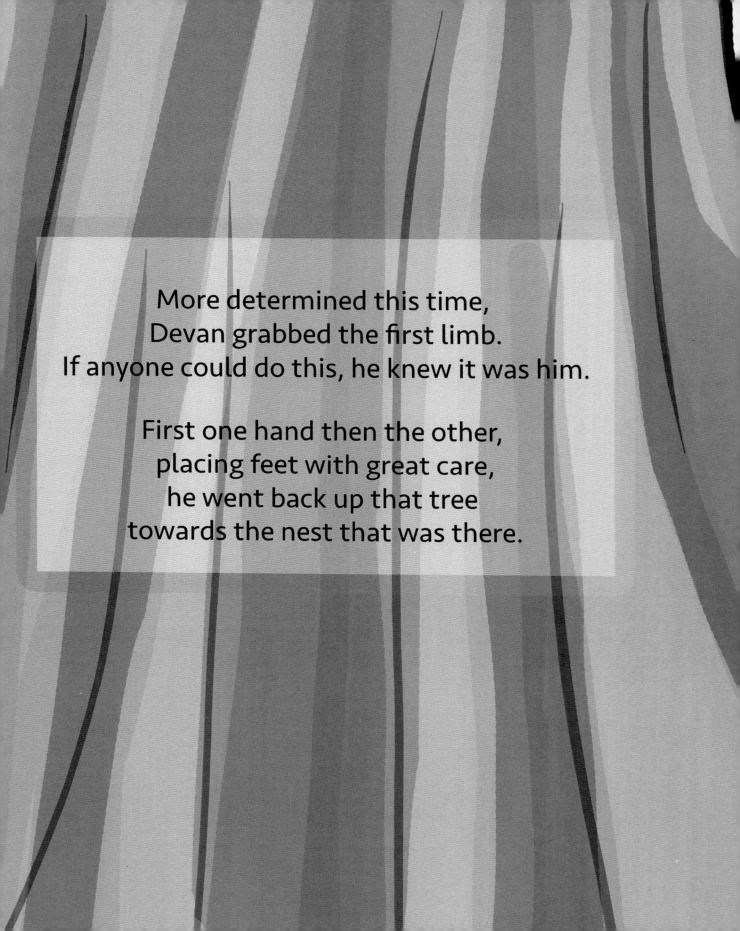

More determined this time,
Devan grabbed the first limb.
If anyone could do this, he knew it was him.

First one hand then the other,
placing feet with great care,
he went back up that tree
towards the nest that was there.

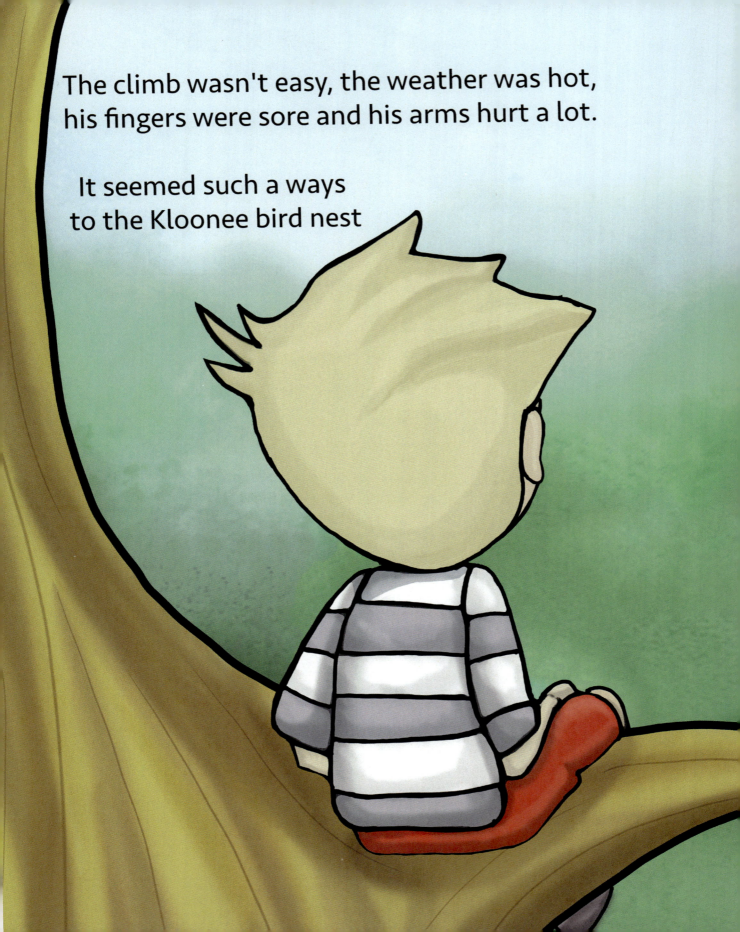

So he sat on a branch for a much needed rest.

And he thought while he sat,
looking down at his friends,
who had gone back to playing their games
without him.

With the aches
in his arms, and the pains in his hands,
he started to question
why he ever began.

"Oh I never will make it,
I'm just wasting my time"

He had worked much too hard
now he just couldn't stop,

So he took a deep breath
and he climbed to the top.

And with every last ounce
of his strength
he reached in

To the nest in the tree,
on the uppermost limb,

Why
did he leave the gold egg in this tree?
And why would he share such a secret
with me?"

As he sat and he thought
in that tree near the top,

He happened to glance
on the valley of Nopp

When the sight that he saw

Nearly made his heart stop…

You had to climb high to behold such a sight,
You had to survive bumps and bruises and fright.

You had to be strong when the battle was hot,
You had to have courage when others did not.
Then all of a sudden the message was clear,
There was more to this climb than the egg lying here.

There was more than just gold and the treasure it brings,

What he learned from his climb was a much greater thing.

Devan now understood
golden eggs are not rare

For as he could see they were found everywhere.

But the treasure of life that is hardest to find
Is a boy, or a girl, with the courage to climb.

And like Devan they learn
that it isn't the Gold,

It isn't the glory or riches untold,
It's the effort
and challenge, it's doing your best,
It's knowing you've conquered
the climb to that nest.

Devan reached in his pocket,
very eager to show
the gold he had found,
so his friends
would all know.

But before he did so
he caught sight of the man,
still holding the cane
in his wrinkly hand.

The man
gave him a look,

A sly smile

And a wink,

Then Devan turned to his friends and said,

"Here's what I think:

If you really want to know what I found in that tree,

Climb up there yourself,

And then you will see."

And around this big tree
	girls and boys like to play.

They play baseball and football
and marbles all day.

		And in the top of that tree
		and the others around,
			Lie pure golden eggs
			waiting there to be found.

		And if you have the courage,
		as did Devan that day,

		You may find your gold egg...
		is just a few bruises away.

From the Author:

My father, Joseph Wyson, was raised in an orphanage from the age of five, having lost both parents. For the next 10 years his physical needs were provided for, but he always yearned for the love and teachings of the parents he did not have. As an adult, he desired to write books for children that might help them learn some of the lessons of life he had missed out on as an orphan. He wrote under the pen name Ule B. Wise, to indicate his desire to teach and inspire. Unfortunately, he passed away before seeing his dream of publishing children's books fulfilled.

I began writing in my youth, beginning with poetry, song lyrics and short stories, followed by hundreds of newspaper columns written in my career as a financial adviser. The inspiration for this children's book came to me early in my marriage as I was starting to build my new business. A recession was going on at the time and a friend questioned the wisdom of starting a business under such difficult circumstances. I responded that "The gold eggs in life are usually found in the nest farthest out on the limb. Those who would have them must be willing to climb out after them, knowing sometimes he may fall, but dusting himself off he climbs up again." And with that, the idea for this book was born. I continued to work on this special story over the next 30 years, with every phase of my life being incorporated into young Devan's climb.

When I finally completed "The Gold Egg," I decided to honor my father by publishing it under his pen name: Ule B. Wise

(Dan Wyson)

Made in the USA
Middletown, DE
14 April 2022